ANIMAL NUMBERS

BERT KITCHEN

DIAL BOOKS

NEW YORK

Answer me this
If you're in the mood,

How many babies
In each mother's brood?

After you pass
Through the counting stage,

The animals' names
Are on the last page.

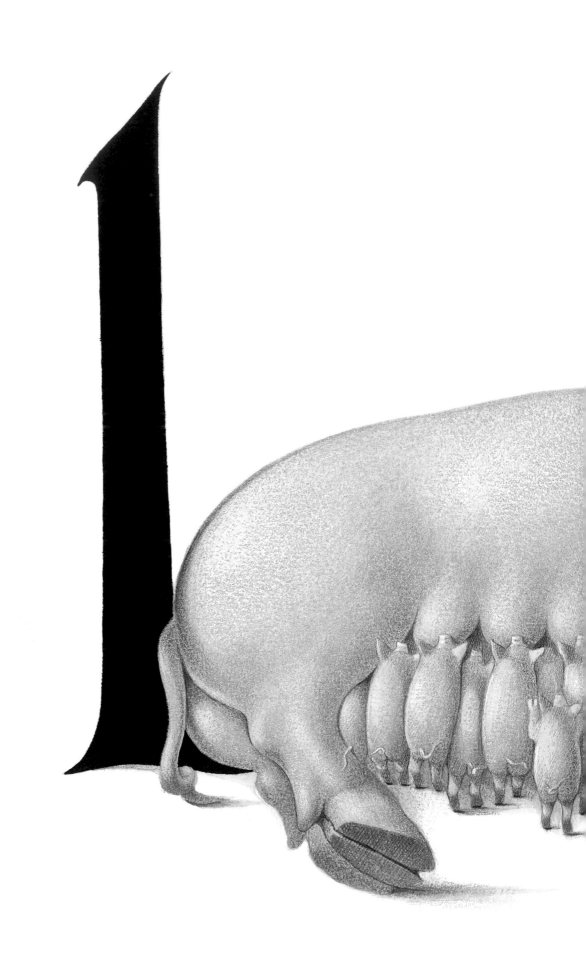

ANIMAL FACTS

1 KANGAROO: The baby kangaroo, or joey, crawls into its mother's pouch immediately after it is born. It stays there for at least 190 days.

2 SWAN: Swans lay 2–5 eggs which hatch into cygnets. These generally swim in close procession behind their mother.

3 SQUIRREL: The babies are born in a hollow or drey in a tree. The young are then reared exclusively by the mother.

4 GREEN WOODPECKER: These birds nest in holes in trees and lay 4–7 eggs. For the first three weeks the parents feed their young on regurgitated food.

5 GREEN LIZARD: The mother lays 4–21 eggs in a hole she digs in the soil. After they hatch she often carries the little lizards around on her back.

6 SHREW: Baby shrews frequently form a long train behind the mother. Each one holds on tightly to the one in front with its teeth.

7 VIRGINIA OPOSSUM: The mother carries her babies on her back. Although she often has more than 7, only those who find space on her back survive.

8 GOLDFISH: The female lays a great many eggs which stick to the water plants. Many of the baby fish die young or are eaten by other fish.

9 SALAMANDER: The yellow blotched salamander lives in moist forests in California. The female lays 7–25 eggs in a burrow or rotting log and guards them until they develop into little salamanders.

10 IRISH SETTER: These elegant dogs have large litters. Extremely energetic, the puppies require lots of exercise and can be trained as game dogs.

15 PIG: Domestic pigs' litters can consist of as many as 20 piglets. The sow is able to feed many of them at once. The smallest piglet is known as the runt.

25 GARTER SNAKE: This snake gives birth to up to 80 fully formed young. They coil around trees and vegetation from an early age.

50 SEA HORSE: Female dwarf sea horses lay at least 50 eggs which are placed in the male's brood pouch. As soon as they hatch the babies can swim.

75 LEATHERBACK TURTLE: The world's largest turtle lays 70–100 eggs in the sand. When they hatch the baby turtles race to the sea to escape predators.

100 COMMON FROG: Though mostly land creatures, frogs breed in water. The female lays up to 30,000 eggs at a time in clusters of frog spawn. These develop into tadpoles and then into frogs.

For Muriel

First published in the United States 1987 by
Dial Books
A Division of Penguin Books USA Inc.
375 Hudson Street
New York, New York 10014
Published in Great Britain by Lutterworth Press
Copyright © 1987 by Bert Kitchen
All rights reserved
Library of Congress Catalog Card Number: 87-5365
Printed in the U.S.A.
First Pied Piper Printing 1991
N
1 3 5 7 9 10 8 6 4 2

A Pied Piper Book is a registered trademark of
Dial Books for Young Readers,
a division of Penguin Books USA Inc.,
® TM 1,163,686 and ® TM 1,054,312.

ANIMAL NUMBERS
is published in a hardcover edition by
Dial Books.
ISBN 0-8037-0910-2